Josh Hartnett

AMERICAN IDOL

LORELEI LANUM

A FIRESIDE BOOK

Published by Simon & Schuster

New York London Toronto Sydney Singapore

FIRESIDE
Rockefeller Center
1230 Avenue of the Americas
New York, NY 10020

Copyright © 2002 by Laura Dail Literary Agency, Inc.
All rights reserved,
including the right of reproduction
in whole or in part in any form.

FIRESIDE and colophon are registered trademarks
of Simon & Schuster, Inc.

For information about special discounts for bulk purchases,
please contact Simon & Schuster Special Sales:
1-800-456-6798 or business@simonandschuster.com

Designed by Joy O'Meara Battista

Manufactured in the United States of America

1   2   3   4   5   6   7   8   9   10

Library of Congress Cataloging-in-Publication Data is available.

ISBN 0-7432-4273-4

CONTENTS

Josh Hartnett

Idol 1. an image, as a statue, worshiped as a deity. 2. Any person or thing devotedly admired. *(The Random House Dictionary)*

Pronunciation: 'ī-dᵊl, function: noun. Etymology: Middle English, from Old French *idole,* from Late Latin *idolum,* from Greek *eidōlon* image, idol; akin to Greek *eidos* form—date: thirteenth century (Merriam Webster online).

"You aspire to be a good person first off and a great actor second. There's no way to go about it. You just draw your own map."

Josh at the Sundance Film Festival, January 2000.

An Idol Is Born

Who doesn't love Josh Hartnett? He is admired, devotedly. He is widely respected. His recent roles playing American soldiers in *Pearl Harbor* and *Black Hawk Down* have moved us to the core. He has conquered demons in *Halloween H2O* and evil aliens in *The Faculty*. In his recent film *40 Days and 40 Nights*, he makes us laugh while he journeys down a religious path to find his inner peace. If you can call giving up all sexual acts (including lovin' himself!) and physical intimacy for Lent a religious path.

While his films have ranged from horror to war to comedy, his characters always have a quiet dignity and a sense of right and wrong. His characters almost always do the right thing. They show self-restraint while performing acts of heroism, both great and small. (Okay, with the glaring exception of his character Hugo in *O*.) These characteristics of Josh's come through, making him a large-screen role model for Americans at home and abroad, whether he's a rebellious teenager or soldier fighting a war on terror. He has something we can all learn from, something that actually makes each of us strive to be a better person.

Maybe the days of the bad boy image are gone. No longer is it cool and hip to be known for boozing it up or partying for days on end. Out are the days of trashing hotel rooms and being "scene." In is being a positive role model, humble and cherishing life. As Josh says, "It's just not chic anymore. 'Moderation' is a pretty big word among the people I know."

In 1999, Josh was voted one of *Teen People* magazine's "21 Hottest Stars under 21." Hollywood.com voted him number 2 on their list of sexiest stars in 2002. But he has also been compared to stars of the 1930s and 40s. He has been said to have the charisma, style, quiet charm, and magnetism of actors like Gary Cooper and Montgomery Clift. Don't remember or know who they are? Well, how about Freddie Prinze Jr.? Some critics and admirers have even called Josh the next Leo DiCaprio, although many disagree—we think Josh's bigger and better.

1

Josh has what so many other stars his age lack—a quiet sense of himself, introspection, a lot of perspective, and the common sense to pay attention to what is happening to his colleagues around him. This star doesn't let fame and looks define him, and he doesn't let himself get carried away by Hollywood. He pays attention to what is happening in the world, and stays grounded by living at home in Minnesota surrounded by family and longtime friends. The combination of these traits and self-confidence will propel him to further success, and deep into everyone's hearts.

Josh played Michael Fitzgerald on the short-lived 1997 ABC series *Cracker*.

The Making of an Idol

Josh, the oldest of four children, was born in San Francisco, California, on July 21, 1978. He has a younger sister, Jessica, and two younger brothers, Jake and Joe, who all grew up together in St. Paul, Minnesota. After their parents' divorce, their mother moved back to San Francisco, and the kids remained in St. Paul with their father, who married Molly, their stepmother. His father used to play guitar for Al Green, and currently is a building manager. His stepmother is a homemaker and artist. Josh says he missed his mom growing up; they didn't really get to know each other very well.

He considers his dad to be a great role model, and has ambitions to follow in his footsteps by being able to put family and important things before his job in order to have a good, full life. Josh says of his dad: "Oh man, he's a great guy. He owns and manages buildings in the Twin Cities, and he's made a life where he rarely has to work too much and he just hangs out with my brothers and sisters. We have a great father."

In St. Paul, Josh attended Nativity of Our Lord School and Cretin-Derham Hall before transferring to South High School. His parents wanted him to go to the same Catholic school they had attended. He had a choice of schools, but they offered to pay only for the school they went to. He hated the uniform, and the conformity. So what did he do? He did what any self-respecting rebellious teenage kid would do. "I defined my character by being the opposite of what the school told me to be," he admitted. "That was unhealthy."

While in high school, Josh played on the football team until a knee injury put an end to his football career. He also swam on the swim team, but that was not enough for him. He wanted to do more with his time and energy.

Encouraged by his aunt, Josh auditioned for a local production company. She convinced him to audition for the role of Huckleberry Finn in Mark Twain's *Tom Sawyer.* He won the lead, and he was only sixteen.

He went on to act in a dozen plays that ran about two weeks each in Minnesota. Some of the produc-

Josh's acting in *Cracker* was so convincing that his father apologized to him for whatever he might have done.

tions were *Freedom Riders* at the Youth Performance Center, *Into the Woods* at Stepping Stone Theater, and *Tom Sawyer* at the Children's Theater Company.

Louise Bormann was the drama director at South High School. Naturally, she remembers Josh: "He was smooth. It was like, 'Whoa! Here's a kid I don't need to coach!'" During a high school production of *Guys and Dolls* in which he played Sky Masterson, a local agent noticed him and immediately handed him a business card. That agent, Nancy Kremer, became his manager. In addition to his theater roles, he also landed a commercial for Mervyn's, a department store.

Josh went back recently to see a final production of Louise's before she transferred to another teaching position. "He hugged me so many times, and he was so excited and wanted to tell me what he was doing." On his success as an actor, she says that he deserves it because he is an honest, hardworking, smart person. "It's as thrilling as can be. I don't think what's happening to him has turned him into someone else. He's just a great kid."

But playing Huck Finn was not Josh's first time on stage, nor was it the beginning of his acting career. His acting career began when he was in grade school, participating as an altar boy at his church, and he learned early to combine acting and making a living: "[We] used to serve at every funeral because we'd get five bucks and we could get out of school. They'd treat it like it was an inconvenience for us. Right. We were like, 'Five bucks, get out of school? It's too bad these people had to die, but they did die; why don't we just serve?' " Okay, so maybe school wasn't his forte; even he says: "I was definitely not a good student."

Which brings us to his run-in with the law. Josh and some of his friends from school were making a video at a local Dairy Queen. They were staging and filming a robbery. One concerned citizen saw the robbery and called the police. Luckily, when the police arrived, the crew was taking a break and having snacks, not holding fake guns. And luckily, the police were understanding, and no one was charged in the mix-up.

While in high school Josh worked at a video store. He watched tons of movies, but didn't necessarily finish them. He was extra picky about which films he would watch. "I'd take home like three or four films a night and at least start them. When you work at a video store, you go, 'That sucks, that sucks, that sucks, that's good, that's not really my taste.' You see so many. Then when you've been in it and you start working on them you realize, 'God, it's hard to make a really brilliant film. It's almost near impossible.' "

He liked *12 Monkeys, The Usual Suspects,* and *Trainspotting,* but his favorite movie was *Basquiat.* Josh loved it "because it combined the New York scene, painting and poetry. Beautifully made, beautifully acted. It's so honest, so spot-on and has such a beautiful message on fame."

Josh graduated from South High School in 1996, and started at the State University of New York at

Purchase (SUNY Purchase) that fall. He was unhappy with life in the acting department at Purchase. Could it have been the endless sight of deadly brown bricks that comprise the aesthetically hostile landscape? Or the nonstop planes roaring overhead? SUNY Purchase is in the direct flight path of the Westchester Airport, located right next door. (A favorite pastime of Purchase students is to climb the fence separating the campus and airport and lie on the runway to watch the planes.) Actually, it was neither. Rumor has it that Josh disagreed with the policies of the acting department and was excused. Josh had been accepted last minute in the acting conservatory, with twenty-five other students. He later found out that the school had funding for only nine of them, so they were pitted against one another in the most vile of internal competitions to see who would get to continue their education and graduate. Josh objected to this process and sent an impassioned letter to the dean. He left after a short while to move to Los Angeles to pursue his acting career. It was February 1997.

We all know that a college education is important; for some it's the key to getting the perfect job. But there are success stories of people who did not finish college, or who were told they would never be successful: Clint Eastwood, Albert Einstein, George Lucas (writer and director of *Star Wars*). The CEO of FedEx, who was given a C on his college paper, his business proposal for FedEx, was told his business would never fly. J. K. Rowling went to twenty-five publishing houses before one would publish her first book, *Harry Potter and the Sorcerer's Stone.* Those are a few success stories; nevertheless, it is a gamble to leave school early. In Josh's case, it just happened to pay off in spades!

Josh would like to go back to school "for history and literature and writing," and he has some regrets about not being the best student, because it closes some doors. "I don't like to not be able to do something. I say if you don't want anybody to ever tell you no in your life, you should just get good grades in high school." I think we can all agree with that!

Josh, in 1997, at the premiere of *U-Turn*, in L.A.

An Idol Path

Just a few months after moving to LA, Josh auditioned for a role in ABC's adaptation of the British detective program *Cracker.* Josh got the part, playing Michael Fitzgerald, the son of Gerry Fitzgerald, played by Robert Pastorelli, who you may or may not remember as the painter on *Murphy Brown.* Gerry was a psychologist with a small practice in a mall. To supplement his income, he lectured at colleges and helped the police solve cases, when wacky issues with his family weren't sidetracking him. Michael was a rebellious, misunderstood teenager. One wonders if Josh was working out some of his own issues from high school. Indeed, his acting was so convincing that his father apologized to him for whatever he had done to Josh when he was in school. Josh said, " 'You didn't do anything—I was acting.' My performance made him feel bad; he had seen those faces before." The show received great reviews, but it could not manage to find an audience. It was aired against the final season of *Seinfeld.* No one was surprised when it was canceled shortly after its first run of nine episodes.

Even though this was a great disappointment to him, he was going on an average of four auditions a day—the average number *per week* for most actors! His agent, Nancy Kremer, says, "The thing is when he went out, every single call, he got a callback on, which is pretty much unheard of. And on top of that, casting directors were calling other casting directors telling them that they should meet him. That's a huge buzz you can't buy in Hollywood. That's just a gift from the heavens."

The cast of *Cracker:* Robert Pastorelli, Carolyn McCormick, Josh Hartnett, Sally Livingston.

Jamie Lee Curtis was an inspiration on the set of *Halloween H2O.*

HALLOWEEN H2O: 20 YEARS LATER

Josh soon landed the role of Jamie Lee Curtis's son in *Halloween H2O: 20 Years Later*. The sequel to the cult classic *Halloween* brings back Michael Myers as the crazed killer brother of Laurie Strode. It pits John Tate, played by Josh Hartnett, rebellious teen son of Keri Tate (Laurie Strode re-invented), and his friends against the killer on Halloween night. Everyone thinks John's mother is going crazy because she has been dreaming about her psycho brother, thinking that he is coming after her. No one believes her, and she is embarrassing John. He refuses to take her seriously, and he and his friends decide to have a Halloween party in the very old, isolated school they attend. Of course it takes place in the basement, and one by one, people are killed off as Michael Myers makes his way to John and Keri Tate.

Josh's role as John Tate won him nominations in 1999, for an MTV Movie Award for Best Breakthrough Performance and for a Blockbuster Entertainment Award for Favorite Male Newcomer. Gaining a role in such a prestigious cult horror classic almost instantly brought him other roles. Soon after *Halloween H2O* he started working on *The Faculty*.

The premiere of Steve Miner's *Halloween H2O*. Josh and Ellen Fenster arrive at Mann's Village Theater.

Shawn Hatosy, Jordana Brewster, Laura Harris, Clea DuVall, and Elijah Wood rounded out the cast of *The Faculty*.

Josh with actress Laura Harris in *The Faculty*.

THE FACULTY

In *The Faculty,* Josh plays Zeke Tyler, a student at Herrington High, Ohio, where a bunch of amphibious aliens start to take over the bodies of the teachers (surely some of us suspected this has always been going on). It's up to this group of high school kids to save the world from being taken over by aliens. But first they have to face problems within their own group, as they start to suspect one another of being invaded by aliens. The only way to tell among his posse of friends who is an alien and who isn't is to snort a powdery substance and to use this to kill the aliens. Not your average method for identifying alien beings! Slowly, methodically, the entire school is being turned into aliens, and the action picks up as the fight for the safety of humankind is on the line.

Josh brings another little-known talent to light in this film. He was not happy with his hair, so he decided to cut it himself! Yes, in this film, he is sporting his own 'do—literally. "I never liked going to the barber, so I cut it myself. The team of people around me gave up on my appearance a long time ago. They know I'm always gonna do the wrong thing as far as appearance goes. It's never not stylish enough to be stylish. They leave me alone." Josh actually auditioned with a hairdo he cut himself. To quote himself as Zeke in the film, "I'm a contradiction."

Josh was nominated by the Academy of Science Fiction, Fantasy and Horror Films for Best Performance by a Younger Actor. Fortune and fame were just around the corner.

Cast of *The Faculty* at Planet Hollywood, NYC.
November 13, 1998.

DEBUTANTE (A.K.A. MODERN GIRL)

Around this time, Josh was also in a short student film called *Debutante* (also known as *Modern Girl*) with Selma Blair (of *Cruel Intentions,* in which she and Sarah Michelle Gellar share a famous female-female kiss, and *The Sweetest Thing*). *Debutante* received some great reviews.

Selma Blair plays Nan, who is on the subway home having flashbacks of her previous night. She had gone to a party with friends (correction, she had snuck out of the house to go to a party with friends), where handsome, sexy Bill, played by Josh Hartnett, tries to seduce her. She totally falls for him, but later at the party she sees him with another girl, spouting the same seducing line. Ah, sometimes guys are such dogs!

THE VIRGIN SUICIDES

Interested in seeing what Josh looks like playing a cool high school kid in the seventies? He sports long hair, large shades, and an attitude that won't quit in *The Virgin Suicides.* The film is the directorial and writing debut of Sofia Coppola, daughter of famous director Francis Ford Coppola.

This is a story about five girls who live in a bizarre home situation in Michigan. Their limited access to the outside world makes them desirable by neighborhood and school boys alike. Trip Fontaine (Josh Hartnett) is the coolest, most sought after boy in school. Trip is interested in the eldest, Lux Lisbon (Kirsten Dunst), but because of her overbearing mother (Kathleen Turner), he must make arrangements to have all the girls attend the prom, so he makes it his personal mission. Mr. Lisbon (James Woods) is the geeky high school math teacher, who doesn't have a clue.

Josh at the 1999 MTV Movie Awards. Santa Monica, California, June 5, 1999.

At the premiere of the film *Happiness* in Los Angeles. January 15, 1999.

Trip Fontaine has a movie star entrance. Outside of school, he is standing next to his car, and as the camera slowly pans up starting from his cool sneakers, to his face, where he sports his pink-tinted large aviator glasses, the song "Magic Man," by Heart, is blasting in the background. Sofia Coppola says about Josh's character, Trip: "We had to make him an icon."

Trip gives Lux a night she will never forget, but unfortunately she misses her curfew, and puts her mother past the point of sanity. The girls undergo lockdown that includes keeping them home from school. Their father can't seem to do anything about it, and he too starts to lose his mind, and then his job. The ending is extraordinary in its unexpectedness. Trip narrates bits and pieces throughout the story as an older man, and we find out that the memory of Lux, as well as of the rest of the sisters, never went away in his mind or in the minds of the other boys.

Josh gives all of himself and more when it comes to defining a role. For this one, he talked to not only the screenwriter, but also the author, Jeffrey Eugenides. Eugenides says, "It was clear he had given a lot of thought to the part. He wasn't taking the thing lightly, and it was gratifying to have one of the actors invest me with the kind of importance, well, the kind of importance writers of novels wish to have over films of their novels. Josh's concentration was also impressive in light of two dozen or so women who were trying to get his attention while we were talking."

O

O began as a screenplay in 1997, but didn't make it onto the big screen until 2001, and with such a short run, it almost went straight to video. While it may not be an Academy Award contender, it has a cast capable of winning Academy Awards, and Josh's acting is something to be seen. *O* was the brainchild of screenwriter Brad Kaaya, and the directorial debut of Tim Blake Nelson (who acted in *O Brother, Where Art Thou?* as Delmar, the mentally challenged convict).

Brad Kaaya's adaptation of William Shakespeare's *Othello* is about sex, drugs, jealousy, violence, and rap. Set in a modern-day elite boarding school, with action-packed competitive basketball scenes, the betrayal unfolds. Josh plays Hugo, based on the original's Iago. He is a jealous, malicious boy who wants only his father's approval. Hugo's father, the school's basketball coach, is played by Martin Sheen (the president on *The West Wing*). His character is the counterpart of Shakespeare's Duke of Venice.

Hugo's goal is to destroy Odin, the sophomore who has his father's eye and heart. Odin (Othello in Shakespeare's play), played by Mehki Phifer, is the talented basketball player who's the hero of the school. He is dating Desi, Julia Stiles's character, based on Shakespeare's Desdemona, and Desi is the daughter of the dean of the school.

Hugo starts out by breaking up Odin's interracial relationship with Desi. Once the seeds of mistrust are sown, conspiracy, betrayal, and violence are not far behind. Hugo is so convincing, methodical, and frighteningly intelligent when it comes to playing everyone against one another. The only person he can't seem to play is his father.

In Josh's words: "It deals with some very disturbing issues that are at the forefront of discussion these days, like school violence and steroids. I think kids can learn from a film like this, use it to explore their ideas and opinions on the subject matter, and heal from their own situations. Just because you don't acknowledge a problem or you forbid a teenager from seeing the movie, it doesn't mean the problem doesn't exist."

Where is Julia Stiles? They went to Sundance together in January 2000.

"Josh has a lot more going on under-neath his appearance than you suspect when you first meet him," said *O* director Tim Blake Nelson.

"It's hard for me to work closely with a girl and not completely fall in love with her as a person," Josh has said.

Josh, at the premiere of *O* on August 27, 2001, in Los Angeles.

Mehki Phifer also spoke out about *O:* "Everything O does is motivated by love, not hate. I hope that the R rating will bring parents and kids to the movie together and bridge some gaps. It should create mutual respect."

Here's a fun fact: Josh and Mehki went to basketball camp together in order to play the heavy basketball scenes. It shows in the movie; the basketball scenes are fantastic. They got game.

THE TRIALS AND TRIBULATIONS OF MAKING *O*

Cast and crew started working in 1997, but the film was not released until 2001. Eric Gitter, one of the producers, was watching dailies when the Columbine High School shooting occurred in Colorado. You probably remember that two students murdered twelve fellow students and one teacher, and wounded twenty-four others. They then killed themselves. The similarities between *O* and the tragedy at Columbine were too close, and it was decided to delay the release of the film to a time when it would not draw on pain or grief, or remind people of the school shooting. They did not want this movie to be associated with what happened in Colorado.

However, the delay was not to be that easy. There were contract violations, contract reneges, lawsuits, political ties, and seven release dates that came and went with no movie. It was finally released August 31, 2001, just eleven days before another tragedy would change American lives forever and would accelerate the release of another of Josh's movies, *Black Hawk Down.*

Josh says of the controversy over *O:*

"I didn't think that Columbine should have affected this film's release as much as it did. It isn't a film that's trying to explain why things like that happen. And we made the film a few months before Columbine happened. At the time it was supposed to shed a little bit of light on that subject. But, then it became such a hot issue. . . . It wasn't meant to teach people. It's a remake of *Othello,* plain and simple. It's a piece of art that I think people should take for art's sake."

O cast members Josh Hartnett, Julia Stiles, and Mekhi Phifer as they arrive at the premiere. August 27, 2001, Los Angeles. A modern teenage adaptation of Shakespeare's *Othello*, the film was delayed for two years after the 1999 shooting deaths at Columbine High School in Colorado.

HERE ON EARTH

Jasper, Josh's character in *Here on Earth,* is in love with Samantha (Leelee Sobieski), his longtime childhood sweetheart. But rich kid Kelly (Chris Klein) comes in and sweeps her away from Jasper. Jasper and Kelly have to spend the summer together after a car race between them levels the diner owned and run by Sam's mother. Their punishment is to rebuild the diner. Kelly lives in an extra room over the garage in Jasper's house. The tension escalates between the two as Kelly can't seem to make any friends, or be nice to anyone in the town, but falls in love with Sam. Sam, who apparently sees something in Kelly that no one else sees, returns his love, creating complications among Sam, Jasper, and the entire town.

Jasper takes the high road (after car crashes, a very sexy brawl between Jasper and Kelly, a shirtless scene, and many sweaty scenes) to help Sam, who has osteosarcoma—bone cancer. Although Jasper is hopelessly in love with Sam, she has fallen in love with Kelly, who decides to desert her during her illness. Jasper tries to persuade Kelly to be with Sam even though it is the last thing he wants. Could it be that Josh's true nature comes through during these final moments, when honor and integrity are the values that shine and prevail?

Here on Earth was actually filmed right after *O,* but released first. How did Josh transition from playing horrible Hugo in *O* to supersweet Jasper in *Here on Earth*? Josh said that playing Jasper "really helped me get out of this. It was tough."

MEMBER

Directed by David Brooks, this is another short film—we're talking sixteen minutes. It is a road tour starring Josh as Gianni. Gianni is driving through Los Angeles looking for the perfect car crash insurance

Josh at the premiere of *Here on Earth*, March 15, 2000.

scam. It has been called densely layered and kaleidoscopic and was shot as one long special effect. Can you believe it took three years to make this sixteen-minute film?

BLOW DRY

Blow Dry, Josh's next film, is a sleeper success. From the creator of *The Full Monty,* it boasts an all-star cast: Rachael Leigh Cook (Josh and Rachael attended the same high school in real life), Alan Rickman (from *Galaxy Quest*—"Never Give Up, Never Surrender!"), Natasha Richardson (who's married to Liam Neeson), Rachel Griffiths from *Six Feet Under,* and supermodel Heidi Klum. Josh plays Brian, the son of retired award-winning hair stylist Phil Allen.

Small-town Keighley is stirred up by the invasion of the British Hairdressing Competition. Keighley is home to once-reigning champion Phil (Rickman). He owns a barber shop with his son Brian. Swooping into town is current champion Ray Roberts, bringing in tow his daughter, Christina (Cook). Christina attended school with Brian (art imitating life?), but then moved to America with her mom. Brian remembers her from a photo taken many years ago. A budding romance begins.

However, Brian's mom, Shelley (Richardson) lives with her girlfriend, Sandra (Griffiths), whom she ran away with. They own a beauty salon just down the street from Phil and Brian. Phil won't talk to either of them; Sandra used to be his model in the hairdressing competitions. Shelley has just found out that her cancer has flared up again and there is nothing the doctors can do. It is her brainchild to get everyone to enter the competition again in order to bring her family together in her last days. Brian, of course, is stuck in the middle of his parents.

Josh doesn't have to look deep within to find motivation for the barber he plays. He's had so much experience cutting his own hair, it makes you wonder if he took this role because of the setting. Do you think he picked up any good haircutting techniques on the set? If he ever gives up acting, he can open his own barber shop.

Giorgio Armani hosted a party for Eric Clapton in June 1999, and Josh turned up. Nothing comes between Josh and his Armani.

Except more Armani.

And except his signature hat.

TOWN & COUNTRY

It seems every actor has a skeleton in his or her filmography. This is Josh's, not that it's his fault. This film had everything it needed to be great—a stellar director and cast (Warren Beatty, Diane Keaton, Andie MacDowell, Garry Shandling, Jenna Elfman, Nastassja Kinski, Goldie Hawn, Josh Hartnett), and a great screenplay—but somehow nothing managed to work. It was supposed to be a black comedy about two middle-aged couples having problems. Porter (Warren Beatty) and Ellie (Diane Keaton) have two children, Tom (Josh Hartnett) and Alice (Tricia Vessey). Porter starts following his wandering eye when it comes to the ladies. Ellie and Porter's friends, another couple, Mona (Goldie Hawn) and Griffin (Garry Shandling) are having problems of their own when Griffin is caught having an affair. Tom and Alice try to deal with their parents' breakup and go on a road trip to find their dad, whom they find in a very compromising position with Auburn (Jenna Elfman).

The Blockbusters and Tough Choices

PEARL HARBOR

On the morning of December 7, 1941, Japanese fighter pilots attacked Pearl Harbor, Hawaii, in what is considered to be the first attack on American soil by enemies. The ferocity and surprise nature of the attack shook the country. At the time of the attack, the president of the United States, Franklin Delano Roosevelt, was in peaceful negotiations with the Japanese prime minister; the United States didn't consider

Josh is joined by *Pearl Harbor*'s producer Jerry Bruckheimer, Kate Beckinsale, Ben Affleck, and the film's director, Michael Bay, on the deck of the USS *John C. Stennis*.

"It will change your life," Jerry Bruckheimer told Josh about making *Pearl Harbor*.

the Japanese an enemy, which made the attack more appalling. More than eleven hundred sailors were killed that day on the USS *Arizona.*

The movie *Pearl Harbor* depicts two young men, played by Ben Affleck and Josh Hartnett. They are friends as children and then join the army together. Rafe (Ben) goes off to be a star fighter pilot for the British air force, and Danny (Josh) gets a cushy station at Pearl Harbor. War, love, personal dilemmas, and a lot of drama define the film.

The actors in *Pearl Harbor* had to attend boot camp. Josh describes his experience: "We did actual army-ranger boot camp, at the army-ranger training grounds. We had actual military guys mixed in with us, and these guys said this was the hardest four days they'd had in the military so far. At the end of it, I wanted to hurt some authority figure really badly. . . . They break you down; they try and make you realize you're absolutely nothing and worth nothing. And then they're supposed to build you back up. Unfortunately, we were only there five days; they didn't have time to build us back up, so we left feeling about as low as we possibly could." But he "learned a lot of respect for the military, which allowed [him] to play [his] character without any sort of cynical edge, which really helped [his] character a lot."

Ben Affleck says of the boot camp, "Just the memory is terrifying. I was doing push-ups, cleaning urinals . . . after a week, I'd have paid ten thousand dollars for a Snickers bar. The other actors wanted me to quit, so then they could quit, too."

Did you know that Josh didn't jump at this role? He thought very carefully about whether he wanted to be a part of a movie that would have the distinction of having the largest budget in moviemaking history. With the scope and size of this production, it was guaranteed to be a hit and draw attention and fame to Josh. For someone who never had any intention of being in the movies, the repercussions of fame were enormous.

"I wasn't actually sure I wanted to be in it. I come from a very liberal background, so I wasn't sure if I wanted to be famous on this kind of level. It seems kind of backward. I don't think it really helps your development as a person, but at the same time it really helps if you're doing the right film."

The cast. Back row, from left: Cary-Hiroyuki Tagawa, Dan Aykroyd, Tom Sizemore, James King, Alec Baldwin, and Colm Feore. Front row: producer Jerry Bruckheimer, Josh Hartnett, Kate Beckinsale, Ben Affleck, Cuba Gooding Jr., and director Michael Bay.

"The truth is, I was really getting into doing roles in smaller movies, so I didn't know if I really wanted to be part of such a huge publicity machine. I wasn't even sure if I wanted to be famous, or anything like that. You know, I had only been making movies for about two years when the possibility of *Pearl Harbor* came along."

"The size of *Pearl Harbor* was one of the scariest things about it. I didn't know if I wanted to do it because the scope was so frightening. I was afraid of the repercussions of fame. I was afraid that everyone would start wanting to know my business, want to sap something out of me, invade my personal life to the point where I [would] have to guard myself against people. That's not my nature. I'm an explorer, but you can't turn down a film because you're worried that the success of it will land you on the cover of every tabloid."

So he discussed the issue with his family, considering the impact it might have on him as well as on them. "The film would change my life and maybe my whole family's, too, and . . . I didn't know if it was the right thing to do. [Dad] said, 'It's your decision. You know regret can be permanent. Fame can be temporary. You can quit and it'll go away anyway. But regret can be permanent.' One of the best things that I said to my dad before I got on the plane to go off and shoot *Pearl Harbor* was 'I'm going to go for a ride until it lets me off.' "

Josh's family had been intimately involved in World War II. His uncle, whom he talked to a lot about the film, was involved in D day and on through the Battle of the Bulge. His uncle was one of the lucky ones; most of his friends were not. "I don't think anybody he knew at the beginning ended up living through it. He wrote letters back all the time, and I read those letters while I was filming this movie. My uncle was a big inspiration for me. He had fought in World War II. He didn't talk that much about it because he said he'd lost all his friends, but he had kept all of the letters he'd received during that period and gave me those letters when he heard that I had gotten the role. He died just as we were starting to film, and I kept reading those letters while we were filming."

Ben Affleck with Josh in *Pearl Harbor*.

Paul Francis, Ewen Bremner, Ben Affleck, Michael Shannon, Alec Baldwin, and Greg Zola starred with Josh in *Pearl Harbor*.

Josh's grandfather was also active in the war during that time, but he was stationed in Italy and North Africa and didn't see action.

Josh interviewed survivors of Pearl Harbor, in addition to reading books about the 1941 attack and World War II. He says of the survivors, "It was meeting the survivors that really made the character come together and made me understand the whole thing better. The thing that stuck in my mind the most was how, after sixty years, they still cry about it."

Even while filming the movie, he remained humble. There were constant challenges. "Trying to find out where I fit in this gigantic thing. The confidence you have to have to feel like you belong on the big screen with all this amazing stuff happening—it's pretty intense. Ben Affleck has that confidence. I tried to reach it while we were shooting."

BLACK HAWK DOWN

"I wanted to work with Ridley, I was excited I could tell friends that I was working with a master! The story never stops being intense, so it's just going to be a wild ride." Director Michael Bay had shown Ridley [Scott] parts of *Pearl Harbor.* Jerry Bruckheimer, who produced *Pearl Harbor,* was also producing *Black Hawk Down.*

Black Hawk Down is based on the book by Michael Bowden, who writes about the horrible failure of U.S. involvement in Somalia on October 3, 1993. This true story takes place in Mogadishu, Somalia. The American soldiers' assignment is simple: kidnap two Somali warlords. The soldiers are given enough firepower to accomplish the mission, and the intelligence for the location of the warlords seems trustworthy. But never have so many things gone wrong.

Josh's character was based on real-life army staff sergeant Matt Eversmann. At the time Staff Sergeant Eversmann was twenty-six years old, with five years experience. He was in charge of a group of

43

twelve men, termed a "chalk." He would lead them into battle. Josh actually met Matt Eversmann at the U.S. Army War College, where Eversmann teaches. The veteran's permanent wounds from the battle in Somalia require him to wear a hearing aid in each ear.

It seems the set was just as intense. At one point during the film shooting, Josh remembers what was going on in his head: "After a while on *Black Hawk,* I wasn't sure where I was anymore. I felt . . . 'Am I still Josh Hartnett?' "

"This is going to sound ridiculous, but we couldn't have any food on the set. We were told that the people of Morocco are so poor that having the food would have caused great fights from people trying to steal it. Even I was like, 'Come on, it's an eighty-million-dollar production.' But the powers in charge also thought all the extras would bring their families to the set to eat, which would have added more to our bottom line.

"The producers thought it might be nice to give the rice away to the locals who were playing extras. But there was an actual, real riot over the rice. It got pretty intense. People went nuts." Josh adds, "It made me feel terrible. You think about how bad some people have it in this world. You feel like this stupid fat cat. . . .

"We had the same haircuts as the actual U.S. military, but I didn't get much outward hatred from the locals. You still felt a little bit like the ignorant white man coming in and wrecking everything for everyone else."

Josh's words at the end of the movie could be the coin phrase for so many people in 2001, when he tells a fallen soldier, "Nobody asks to be a hero. It just happens that way."

"It's the first movie I've been in that I want my friends to see. I'm usually so embarrassed—by my performance and just being in movies—but this one is almost necessary to watch," Josh has said. And it's true: *Black Hawk Down* is an intense, emotion-evoking chronicle that was a contender for the 2002 Oscars.

While in Africa, Josh expressed interest in volunteering for Habitat for Humanity, an organization that helps build homes for the needy in eighty countries across the globe. He wanted to travel through Africa and assist where he could. Building a diner in the movie *Here on Earth* may have sparked an affinity for con-

7. DEZEMB
ES GESCHAH AN EINEM

"Hugging girls is second nature to me."

Josh, who stars with Ben Affleck as U.S. Army Air Corps buddies in the movie *Pearl Harbor*, waves as he arrives for the world premiere, which was on the deck of the U.S. Navy aircraft carrier USS *John C. Stennis*, May 21, 2001. Thousands of Navy personnel and guests attended the premiere.

struction, in addition to his desire to help people. Are you interested in helping? Check out www.habitat.org, and find out what you can do.

.

40 DAYS AND 40 NIGHTS

This movie was actually filmed between *Pearl Harbor* and *Black Hawk Down,* but due to the events on September 11, its release was delayed. That seems to be a theme with Josh's films.

Matt (Josh's character) works for a design company, in a very cool office space in San Francisco. The movie opens with him filming his current love, Nicole (played by Vinessa Shaw). She dumps him. This is the beginning of his downward spiral into chaos and uncertainty.

He goes on a dating and sleeping spree with women, with the help of his roommate, played by Paulo Costanzo, who always has a connection to the "next party." But then, as Matt is caught in flagrante delicto, his world is rent apart with a giant rift forming in the ceiling. It's all in his mind, of course, but this starts to pose problems and tension with his date of the moment.

He begins to discuss his troubles with his older brother, played by Adam Trese (a SUNY Purchase grad). His brother is studying to be a priest but, unbeknownst to Matt, is having his own problems with the whole celibacy issue involved in joining the church.

Matt decides to give up sex for Lent. This includes self-gratification, intimacy, and all sexual acts. This means he needs to get rid of all vices and items that will lead him into temptation. His vast and, to some, enviable collection of porn videos, magazines, assortment of sexual toys, and sexual aids must go. He must have had to take out a separate storage unit to hold all of it!

Unfortunately, he can't get rid of women. His office finds out about his Lent promise, via his roommate, and a betting pool is born, complete with website and contributors from as far away as Asia. His model-gorgeous female coworkers try to corrupt his conviction throughout the movie, and we watch the sad

"He'll act surprised if people want his autograph. He's real modest. I don't know if he really believes he's a star," said *Pearl Harbor* costar William Lee Scott.

but hysterically funny breakdown of Matt. By the last week, he has the shakes, is seeing naked women wherever he goes, and is having to give his very-male member an ice bath to calm it down!

Did I mention that during his first week he meets the love he has been looking for, but he's now unable to pursue her due to his decision to observe Lent? Erica, played by Shannyn Sossamon, is the sensitive, real, beautiful young woman that has his interest.

Josh with a friend at a party at the Sundance Film Festival in Park City, Utah. January 28, 2000.

However, comedy isn't all humor, naked women, and sex. There's pain, too. Josh is chained to the bed to get him through his last hours of Lent. Did he like being chained up? "That was NOT a good day. I'm not into that bondage sh—. I think I spent a couple of days chained there. My wrists were all raw and cut up—they were real handcuffs. They had a little bit of fur on them, a little bit of padding, but it didn't help." Did Josh learn nothing from his army training camp?

Did you know that Josh tried to get into his character by imitating Matt's abstinence? Josh admitted he lasted only about two and a half weeks, and as he jokingly said, "It was the self-gratification clause that finally did me in." No pun intended, right?

"The script scared the hell out of me because when I started reading it, I realized, 'Goddamn it, it's a sex comedy. This is brilliant. They'll never make it because it's so sexual.' "

"Comedy was hard for me—to try and figure out how to go about making something funny. In comedy, you have to have good humor about your pain. Even the character himself has to be able to recognize the humor. The director told me sometimes to cool off and relax, that it's really not the end of the world. He said that this character, he can't be humorless, and I took it to heart."

Does this film objectify women? "There are so many films that objectify women. In this one, the women are the only sane characters. Sometimes the nature of sexual thoughts doesn't come in a 'Boy, I would really like to get to know that person as a whole person' kind of way."

Present and Future Idol

Josh has been working hard. He's made twelve movies since he started acting in 1997. That year, Miramax offered him a four-movie contract, a great start for any actor. He fulfilled that contract with the release of *40 Days and 40 Nights.* His other films released for Miramax are *H2O,* his first film; *The Faculty, Blow Dry,* and *O. O* was purchased by Miramax after it had been filmed, so it was not considered part of the contract. What is he going to do now?

"I'm going to take some time off after this one *[40 Days and 40 Nights]. Pearl Harbor* and *Black Hawk Down* were two big movies. I wear uniforms in both. I didn't want to do another epic war drama. I don't want all this to make me flip my lid. I feel lucky. I'm grateful. But I must keep my balance. And try not to be too cynical. . . . The one good experience is, if you make it, filmmakers become more willing to put money behind your movie. That's the great part."

Okay, before you panic, we will be able to see Josh next in *The Rum Diaries,* which is based on the book by journalist Hunter S. Thompson. It will also star Benicio Del Toro and Johnny Depp. Michael Thomas will write the script for the movie, and FilmEngine's Anthony Rhulen will produce it. It starts shooting in the winter of 2003.

Not one to sit idle, Josh has started his own production company, Roulette Entertainment, with Elden Henson (formerly known as Elden Ratliff, he played Roger Rodriguez in *O* and he was in *Cheaters*). We can't wait to see the projects they produce.

Josh says he is moving to New York City. Where? When? He'll have to leave the Minnesota Vikings at home, as New Yorkers are not the most tolerant people when it comes to errant sports fans! Even former mayor Rudy Giuliani, NYC hero and diehard Yankee fan, gets booed at Shea Stadium (home of the Mets). But *nothing* beats the New York City spirit, not even terrorist attacks. Josh will fit right in and hopefully feel right at home.

"I'm at a point in my life where everything is a struggle. You're not quite an adult, you're not quite a kid. You're in that strange, extended adolescence when you don't know what to make of the world. So I'm choosing roles that shed some light on that. I'm just going by whatever comes. I'm trying my hand at everything—just dabbling. We'll see how it works out."

Josh watched the 2000 Academy Awards at *Vanity Fair*'s Oscar party at Morton's restaurant.

53

Idol Facts

THE STATS

Josh's birthday is July 21, 1978 (Cancer), born in San Francisco, California. He grew up, as you know, in St. Paul, Minnesota. He is 6'3", with brown, soulful eyes, and brown hair that is almost always covered with a cap! He weighs 163, and will be twenty-four on July 21, 2002.

He just bought a house in Minneapolis. He lives with bats in the attic—he says he can't get them out.

He is dating Ellen Fenster, longtime sweetheart from home, and who is understanding of the bats.

He is Roman Catholic.

HIS BIG BREAKS

His first acting role was playing Huck Finn in Mark Twain's *Tom Sawyer*.

He was discovered while playing Sky Masterson in a high-school production of *Guys and Dolls*.

Nancy Kremer became his agent. She specialized in bringing talent from the Twin Cities in Minnesota to Hollywood.

He landed a national Northwest Airlines commercial, and a commercial for Mervyn's, a Minnesota department store.

In Hollywood, he landed a role on ABC's American version of a British detective show called *Cracker*. He played Michael Fitzgerald, a rebellious, troubled teenager.

Josh's next role was in his first film, *H2O*, a bona fide horror classic.

Who's with Josh at the *Vanity Fair* party? It's Leelee Sobieski.

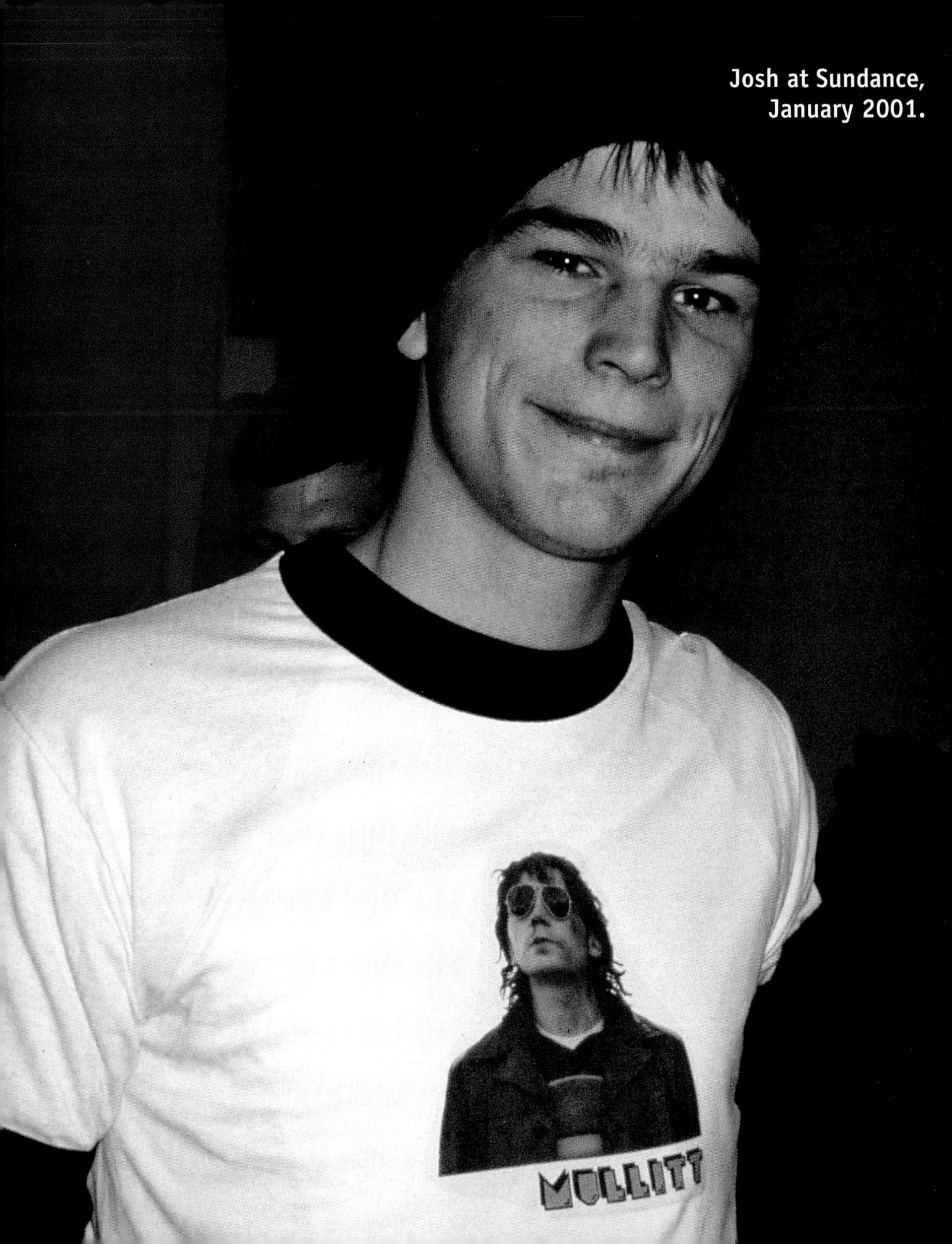

Josh at Sundance,
January 2001.

His blockbuster films include *Pearl Harbor* and *Black Hawk Down*.

His first stand-alone film is considered to be *40 Days and 40 Nights*, a comedy.

AWARDS AND NOMINATIONS

2002: Won ShoWest Award for Male Star of Tomorrow at ShoWest Convention USA.

2002: Nominated for the Razzie Award for worst screen couple for *Pearl Harbor;* he shares this nomination with Ben Affleck and Kate Beckinsale.

Seventeen magazine named him unofficial "Hottie of the Year" after his performance in *The Faculty.*

Nominations in 1999 for an MTV Movie Award for Best Breakthrough Performance and for a Blockbuster Entertainment Award for Favorite Male Newcomer for his performance in *Halloween H20.*

Josh was also nominated by the Academy of Science Fiction, Fantasy and Horror Films for Best Performance by a Younger Actor.

IDOL RUMORS

He did not audition for *Dawson's Creek* six times.

He is not an alcoholic—and please don't spread nasty rumors like that, as he doesn't want his grandmother to read about them!

He and Julia Stiles are just friends. (Uh-huh. Even though they went to her prom together.)

He only worked in the video store to make money and get free videos, not because he wanted to become an actor.

He did not *rob* a Dairy Queen; he was making a film. He and his crew were eating candy bars when the police showed up.

IDOL THOUGHTS

He doesn't wear underwear. Keep that in mind the next time you see him. . . .

Josh once referred to himself as *boring* to *Cosmo Girl*!

He considers himself to be a "scrawny thing," and not sexy.

He wears a knit cap (which he is never without) and used to cut his own hair.

He cut his own hair for the movie *The Faculty*.

He's a committed Minnesota Vikings fan.

He was in the music video "Playground" by the band Air, for the motion picture soundtrack of *The Virgin Suicides*.

He likes to listen to music: "What I listen to depends on the scene, but it's the easiest way to wrap my head around an emotion. Right now it's [Bob] Dylan, [Bob] Marley, Miles Davis, the Beastie Boys, Tom Waits, and the Velvet Underground." His favorite types of music are blues and jazz.

The Beats had the biggest literary influence on him when he was young.

He recently donated money to a Buddhist temple in Minneapolis.

He has dated supermodel Gisele Bundchen and been "associated" with actresses Monet Mazur, Izabella Miko (she was in *Coyote Ugly*), Michelle Williams, and girl from home Kelly Lee Carlson, but these are just rumors!

He is now dating Ellen Fenster, longtime love from St. Paul. But don't worry—he says he is not ready to settle down, so don't give up hope!

The greatest influences in his life are his family, from his aunt who pushed him into acting, to his father, about whom he says "We [his brothers and sister] have a great father."

He has had to attend two army-training boot camps for his roles in *Pearl Harbor* and *Black Hawk Down*. That's a lot of army training for one actor.

58

On February 1, 2001, Josh turned out for an industry screening of *Hannibal* in Mann Village, California.

Josh outside the VH1/Vogue Fashion Awards in New York City. October 19, 2001.

And inside the 2001 VH1/Vogue Fashion Awards.

Actors Ewan McGregor, left, William Fichtner, center, and Josh pose for photographers at the premiere of *Black Hawk Down*. Tuesday, December 18, 2001, in Beverly Hills, CA.

The highlight of being on the set of *40 Days and 40 Nights*? When author Lawrence Ferlinghetti visited. "The only time I saw Josh really light up," says Michael London, the producer.

His literary hero is Jack Kerouac. His favorite book while in high school was *On the Road* because it "made [him] want to see the world."

The character he relates most to is Huck Finn, in *Tom Sawyer.* "I have wanderlust. A need to keep going. A hunger to move around, see things, learn. When I was fourteen, I began to read a lot of Kerouac—*On the Road, Dharma Bums, Big Sur.* I always wanted to get out and see what was there."

The life he would have if he could is Eric Idle's, because "I grew up on *Monty Python and the Holy Grail.*" Eric Idle is a writer, actor, composer, and producer. He wrote many of the sketches for the series *Monty Python's Flying Circus,* a terribly funny British television show, and contributed to the screenplays of the films *Monty Python and the Holy Grail, Life of Brian,* and *Monty Python's Meaning of Life.* Not familiar with Monty Python? Go out and rent *Monty Python and the Holy Grail,* episodes of *Monty Python's Flying Circus,* or *Life of Brian.* Nice choice; original, too.

Josh drives a silver Audi A4, although he first looked at a Volkswagen. He really wants a Toyota Land Cruiser. "It's just this big box on wheels. It looks like a really big, wedgy mail truck. It's just a cool truck. And it's got so much power to it, I could drag my house along if I really ever wanted to get a house." (He's got a house, complete with bats in the belfry or attic.)

Josh has the same birthday as Robin Williams, William S. Burroughs Jr., Ernest Hemingway—and Don Knotts!

Josh On

LOST LOVE:

"I've had my heart broken, and it's not fun. But I'd rather have my heart broken than break someone else's heart."

HIS FIRST TIME IN LOVE:

"I think [it was] when I was sixteen. Yeah. It was pretty intense . . . [but] love always changes. It's too ambiguous. For some people it's not. They know exactly what it is. Uh . . . I think that's what a lot of life is, what confidence is: just convincing yourself you have an answer that works. Finding those things for yourself, structuring like, your emotions."

WOMEN:

"English girls are difficult; you never know where you stand. Australian girls are merciless; they just throw themselves on you. French girls are a hit. No matter what they look like, as soon as I hear their accent, I can't resist."

"I look for something different in a girlfriend: something surprising that I haven't seen before. If a girl doesn't have a sense of humor, then what would we talk about? Looks are important, but a sense of humor is more important."

The LA premiere of *Black Hawk Down*. Beverly Hills, CA, December 18, 2001.

Josh plays the role of Army Staff Sgt. Matt Eversmann in *Black Hawk Down*.

Josh stops for photographers as he arrives for the premiere of *Black Hawk Down*, January 15, 2002, at the Uptown Theatre in Washington.

"I hate when girls take forever to get ready. I find that really annoying, and I don't understand how they can take so much time for all that preparation. I just wouldn't be able to spare all that time."

"Women are a mystery. I've never been able to figure one out. But it's a lot more fun to go to work with a beautiful, intelligent, exciting woman than it is to go to work with a bunch of middle-aged men. No offense to the middle-aged men of the world."

RELATIONSHIPS:

"I'm looking forward to the excitement that comes with sharing your life with one person, instead of throwing it all out to the wind or keeping it all to yourself. But I couldn't handle it at this point, I'm too immature."

HE CAN LEAVE HIS CAP ON! ON TAKING HIS CLOTHES OFF:

"That wouldn't come into question for me. My body isn't really in shape because I go to the gym at best one time a year."

MISSED OPPORTUNITIES:

Josh has lost some parts to Heath Ledger, whom he considers his most direct competition for movie roles.

"*Ten Things I Hate About You* wasn't a role I was dying to get, but it wasn't a role I didn't want, either.

69

I was sent the script for *The Patriot,* and I didn't read it because I was shooting another movie. Once I read it, I thought it was great, but by the time I called, Heath Ledger was already cast. My biggest problem is that I don't read the scripts on time. That's me, a day late and a dollar short."

HIMSELF:

"I hope I'm a caring person. I think I'm a genuinely mixed-up person. I'm aware of being goofed-up and just happy to be going through it. I'm a guy who likes to explore. I'm just looking for the next adventure."

HIS SECRET HOBBY:

He paints because it relaxes him, because it's just him "and the canvas, and there's no right or wrong way."

HIS INSPIRATION:

Jamie Lee Curtis was an inspiration on the set of *H20.* Also Marlon Brando, Paul Newman, Cary Grant, James Dean, and Jimmy Stewart; stars that have passed the test of time.

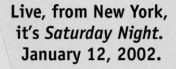

Live, from New York, it's *Saturday Night*. January 12, 2002.

Hosting *Saturday Night Live* was one of the highlights of his year. January 12, 2002.

STARDOM AND FAME:

"In life terms it's been okay, it's a give and take. It's made it a lot easier to get good projects coming around. I was getting good scripts before, but we couldn't get them made into movies because it wasn't commercially viable and so that's changing."

"But I've got people sitting on their cars and looking in my windows in front of my house, and that's a little weird."

"I never paid any attention to that [his being a star] because I know that's not the case. All the stuff that has led up to this is based on decisions I've made and luck that I've had. All I want to do is make good movies. If you read the articles, you get a big head, which upsets me. I'd get really angry with myself if I started acting like that. The only other reaction is to get pissed off because someone doesn't like you. So it doesn't help me at all, so I stay away from it. I try not to pay attention to it and just hang out with my family and friends."

"I love to reach out and slot myself into the Hollywood system and do my own thing, but I don't ever want to be a fully fledged member—someone who is in a stable environment. I don't want to be a pillar. I wanna be the guy on the outside hitting it with a hammer."

"Fame can just snatch you up. Suddenly, it's beyond your control. Feelings of jealousy, of envy, can separate your friends from you. You, in turn, can get nasty, get scared of your friends—scared that they're out to take something from you. You can lose sight that your friends have been your friends for a long time and they don't want anything from you except your friendship."

"If you're going on the freeway, you get to the place you want to a lot quicker, but you don't get to see the surrounding area. I've taken the side streets pretty much my whole life, so hopefully that'll keep working out."

"I don't plan on changing the way I live." (on the sudden fame that *Pearl Harbor* brought)

Ben Affleck says, "[Josh] has exposed his name to people all over the world. The guy will have beautiful women camped out on his front lawn for months."

Josh signed autographs outside the Ed Sullivan Theatre when he did *Late Night with David Letterman* again on January 14, 2002.

Did Dave convince Josh to move to New York City?

Can Josh learn about fame from Ben? "I don't know if I could learn anything from Ben or anyone else until it happens, but I think Ben's holding together very well. I've seen other people who aren't. I do know that when you're not famous you're trying to find exciting things to happen in your life, and when you're famous there's always something coming at you. There's never a dull moment. So I figure when you're very famous, you look for dull moments."

HUMILITY:

He still doesn't think he's famous! "People come up a lot more and want to talk to me. I'm still waiting to deal with it; I don't know when it's gonna become intolerable, 'cause I hear a lot of stories and I see where it becomes too much. But I don't really go to the spots . . . if I lived here and went to Hollywood-type parties a lot, but I don't do that. Unless people follow me back to Minnesota, which would be their loss 'cause my friends and family would destroy them. Minnesota people are very polite. They treat you like a normal human being. I guess it's been good for me to be back there. I feel pretty much in a good spot."

Josh Dishes on Costars and Colleagues:

Mekhi Phifer in *O:*

"Mekhi and I got along very well. We went to this basketball camp together for three weeks where we got the tools to make the basketball scenes come to life. [We] both sunk our teeth in. We never played one-on-one or anything, but Mekhi's not that competitive a guy. He's just a real good guy. He liked to say, 'That's love, man.' We got along really well."

Jerry Bruckheimer, producer of *Black Hawk Down* and *Pearl Harbor:*

"Jerry has been nothing but good to me."

Ridley Scott, director of *Black Hawk Down:*

"Ridley is such a masterful world-maker, catching these details—like the man near the beginning of the film, praying with the AK (Kalashnikov rifle) at his side. That suddenly brings you into the world that we're in. We have a real problem of being ignorant on a lot of world politics, being so self-contained. But I think we need to pay attention to what's happening in the world, because, obviously, a lot of people are unhappy with us.

"Ridley is so about what he's doing at every given moment that he needs to be stolen—people keep stealing Ridley and taking him somewhere else. Like his girlfriend steals him and says, 'Be with me, be home for a while,' and Bruckheimer steals him, puts him back in the editing bay. He never leaves there for twenty-five hours. . . . He's so much about what's happening right in front of him, so present. And that's pretty cool to see."

76

Actress Kate Hudson and Josh, backstage, after presenting an award at the Fifty-ninth Annual Golden Globe Awards in Beverly Hills, California. Sunday, January 20, 2002.

Black Hawk Down director Ridley Scott presented Josh with the Male Star of Tomorrow Award at the ShoWest Gala. Thursday, March 7, 2002, at the Paris Hotel and Casino in Las Vegas.

Tom Sizemore, costar in *Pearl Harbor* and *Black Hawk Down*:

"[He has a] . . . wild energy—he harnesses it and lets it explode onscreen."

Ben Affleck, costar in *Pearl Harbor*; Josh talks about Ben's entering rehab:

"Whenever anything like this comes up, it makes me count my blessings and take stock of my life. Ben's experience is something I can take to heart. There are many temptations out there. It's not like this fame thing is easy, and Ben must have had it twice as bad as I did. You lose all your perspective. Being with the people that I've known since childhood helped me regain a sense of perspective.

"I got on really well with Ben, but his reputation preceded him; for me at least, [it] was that he was a real dick. So many people told me he was an arrogant bastard. When I met him, he totally threw me for a loop. He's the most down-home, together guy. Really, really intelligent and very, very funny to be around."

Benicio Del Toro:

"When I saw Benicio Del Toro do such a fantastic job in *Traffic*, I thought, 'Come on, all it is is a series of facial movements. Why can't I make my face do what Benicio's does?' He's unbelievable."

Michael Bay, director of *Pearl Harbor*:

"He's really passionate and feels he hasn't figured out a different way to get things done quickly other than getting really hard on people. The stuff that he pulled off while we were shooting was amazing, so I felt lucky to be around that kind of visual genius."

Black Hawk Down director Ridley Scott holds his nominee's plaque for Outstanding Directorial Achievement in Feature Films alongside Josh, backstage at the Directors Guild Awards in Los Angeles, Saturday, March 9, 2002. Alas, director Ron Howard won in the category for *A Beautiful Mind*.

On Josh

Michael Lehmann, director of *40 Days and 40 Nights:*

"But even while doing comedy, Hartnett's seriousness and earnestness as an actor show through. It's tough, I don't know if he realized when he got into it how much work and how difficult it is when you show up to do comedy. . . . I think he put more pressure on himself than any other actor I've ever worked with. He approaches a role like everything depends on it. I sensed a seriousness in his method, even when what we were doing seemed a little silly."

Mark Piznarski, director of *Here on Earth:*

"He could do anything and look good. [He considers Josh to be one of the most gifted actors.] A throwback to guys like Brando and Dean—the way they really internalize the difficulties and the pain the character is going through. He just comes off in such a wholesome, realistic way."

Jerry Bruckheimer, producer of *Black Hawk Down* and *Pearl Harbor:*

"Similar to Gary Cooper, he has a quiet, magnetic presence that draws audiences in. You cannot help but like him. Both onscreen and off, he captures your attention and keeps you engrossed in the characters he portrays."

 81

Ridley Scott, director of *Black Hawk Down:*

Josh has "a fundamental maturity and common sense that will take him a long way. He's essentially a kid, about the same age as my daughter. I can remember when I was twenty-three. To be thrown into that degree of success so quickly is a lot to handle, and he does it really well."

Ben Affleck, co-hottie in *Pearl Harbor:*

"I think he struggled with *Pearl Harbor* and *Black Hawk Down* in terms of the military themes and the fear that those films would veer into jingoistic, rah-rah nonsense."

Shannyn Sossamon, costar in *40 Days and 40 Nights* (about Josh and Heath Ledger):

"[Being famous] just shocks them. They're just cool guys who want to hang out, watch movies, and cook with friends. I don't think they get off on it [at] all."

William Lee Scott, costar in *Pearl Harbor:*

"Women definitely react to him. The dude's like six three—a big, tall, strapping, good-looking movie star. He'll act surprised if people want his autograph. He's real modest. I don't know if he really believes he's a star. It hasn't fully settled in."

"I don't think what's happening to him has turned him into someone else. He's just a great kid," said his high school theater director, Louise Bormann.

Josh at the premiere of *40 Days and 40 Nights*, at the Festival Theatre in Westwood, California.

Farewell and Good Luck!– Or, Break a Leg

When he left Minnesota to embark on his acting career, Josh said, "I'm gonna see how far I can ride this thing."

"It's been quite a wild ride for me, I've just been so lucky. I'm still not certain that I comprehend what is happening to me right now, and I certainly have no real grasp of what could happen to me down the line. For now, I'll just wait and see. . . ."

This star is rising.

HOW WELL DO YOU KNOW JOSH? TAKE OUR QUIZ AND TEST YOUR KNOWLEDGE

1. What was Josh's first play?

2. Name two *other* plays Josh was in while still in high school in Minnesota.

3. Josh:

    (a) is the youngest of two brothers and one sister

    (b) has a twin sister and two brothers

    (c) is the oldest of two brothers and one sister

    (d) is an only child

4. Name one of his two short films.

5. Name one of Josh's favorite movies.

6. Name one of his favorite authors.

7. Name one of his favorite books.

8. What is Josh never without?

9. What is Josh always without?

10. Identify the following quote: "Nobody asks to be a hero. It just happens that way."

11. Who's prom did Josh attend?

12. What movie was made in Sale, Morocco?

13. What rumors would Josh like to clear up?

   (a) He's an alcoholic.

   (b) He auditioned for *Dawson's Creek* six times.

   (c) He's dating/dated Julia Stiles.

   (d) He worked in a video store because he wanted to become an actor.

   (e) All of the above

14. Which actor does he consider to be his most serious competition?

   (a) Ben Affleck

   (b) Tom Sizemore

   (c) Heath Ledger

   (d) Leonardo DiCaprio

15. Which character does he most identify with?

   (a) Michael Fitzgerald

   (b) Staff Seargent Matt Eversmann

   (c) Huck Finn

   (d) Hugo

16. Which movies turned Josh down for plum roles?

   (a) *Good Will Hunting*

   (b) *The Talented Mr. Ripley*

   (c) *The Thin Red Line*

   (d) *The Patriot*

17. What movie did Josh cut his own hair for?

   (a) *The Faculty*

   (b) *Halloween H2O: 20 Years Later*

   (c) *Black Hawk Down*

   (d) *40 Days and 40 Nights*

18. Name three people who share a birthday with Josh (but not necessarily the same year).

19. For which movie did Josh almost not take the role?

   (a) *Halloween H2O*

   (b) *Member*

   (c) *O*

   (d) *Pearl Harbor*

   (e) *Blow Dry*

20. Name four enemies Josh's characters have battled in his films.

At the world premiere of *40 Days and 40 Nights*.

87

1. *Tom Sawyer*

2. *Guys and Dolls, Freedom Riders, Into the Woods*

3. C

4. *Member* or *Debutante*

5. *Basquiat, Trainspotting, 12 Monkeys, Usual Suspects*

6. Jack Kerouac

7. *On the Road*

8. His cap

9. Underwear!

10. Staff Sergeant Matt Eversmann said this to a fallen soldier at the end of *Black Hawk Down*. A very poignant phrase.

11. Julia Stiles

12. *Black Hawk Down*

13. E

14. C

15. C

16. B and C

17. A

18. Ernest Hemingway, Robin Williams, Don Knotts, William S. Burroughs Jr.

19. D

20. Evil aliens, Somali warlords, psycho killers, Japanese soldiers

FILMOGRAPHY

1997 *Cracker* (ABC television series). Directed by Stephen Cragg, Tucker Gates, Whitney Ransick, James Steven Sadwith. Produced by James Steven Sadwith, Scott M. Siegler. Written by Jimmy McGovern. Josh plays Michael Fitzgerald, troubled rebellious teen.

1998 *Halloween H2O: 20 Years Later*. Directed by Steve Miner. Produced by Paul Freeman. Screenplay by Robert Zappia and Matt Greenberg, based on characters created by Debra Hill and John Carpenter. Josh plays John Tate. A Dimension Film.

1998 *The Faculty*. Directed by Robert Rodriguez. Produced by Elizabeth Avellan and Robert Rodriguez. Story by David Wechter and Bruce Kimmel. Screenplay by Kevin Williamson. Josh plays Zeke Tyler. A Dimension Film.

1998 *Debutante/Modern Girl*. Written and directed by Mollie Jones. Produced by Laura Branosky, Michiko Byers, Lindsey Cline. With Selma Blair as Nan. Josh plays Bill.

1999 *The Virgin Suicides*. Written and directed by Sofia Coppola in her directorial debut. Produced by Francis Ford Coppola. Based on the novel by Jeffrey Eugenides. Josh plays Trip Fontaine.

2000 *Here on Earth*. Directed by Mark Piznarski. Produced by David T. Friendly. Written by Michael Seitzman. Josh plays lovesick Jasper Arnold.

2001 *Member*. Directed by David Brooks. Produced by Juan Carlos Alvarez, James Kendrew, Gilbert Mercier, and Don Tardino. Josh plays Gianni.

2001 *Blow Dry*. Directed by Paddy Breathnach. Produced by David Rubin, William Horberg, and Ruth Jackson. Written by Simon Beaufoy. Starring Rachael Leigh Cook and Josh Hartnett. He plays Brian.

2001 *Town & Country*. Directed by Peter Chelsom. Produced by Andrew Karsch, Fred Roos, and Simon Fields. Written by Michael Laughlin and Buck Henry. A New Line Cinema Film. Josh plays Tom Stoddard.

"He's earth-shatteringly handsome in a slightly surprised way—he can't quite believe when everyone is falling over him and teasing him about being so good-looking." —Kate Beckinsale

91

"Whoa! Here's a kid I don't need to coach," Louise Bormann, Josh's high school theater director, said.

Josh at the ShoWest Awards Ceremony, March 7, 2002, Paris Hotel, Las Vegas.

2001 *Pearl Harbor*. Directed by Michael Bay. Produced by Jerry Bruckheimer. Written by Randall Wallace. With Ben Affleck, Kate Beckinsale, and Josh Hartnett. Josh plays Captain Danny Walker. A Touchstone Picture.

2001 *O*. Directed by Tim Blake Nelson. Based on William Shakespeare's *Othello*. Screenplay by Brad Kaaya. Produced by Anthony Rhulen. Starring Mehki Phifer, Josh Hartnett, Julia Stiles. Lion's Gate Entertainment. Josh plays Hugo Goulding. Film actually shot in 1997.

2001 *Black Hawk Down*. Directed by Ridley Scott. Produced by Jerry Bruckheimer. Written by Mark Bowden. Screenplay by Ken Nolan. Starring Josh Hartnett and Ewan McGregor. Josh plays Staff Sergeant Matt Eversmann.

2002 *40 Days and 40 Nights*. Directed by Michael Lehmann. Produced by Michael London. Written by Rob Perez. Josh plays Matt Sullivan.

BIBLIOGRAPHY

Black Hawk Down—A Story of Modern War, Mark Bowden. A Signet Book, New York, 2000

Chicago Sun Times, September 6, 2001

Cosmo Girl, April 2002

Cosmopolitan, June 2001

Dish, June 2001

Upon reflection, a thoughtful actor.

Empire, June 2001

Entertainment Weekly, February 21, 2002; September 2001

In Style, April 2000

Interview, January 1999

Movieline Magazine, June 2001

New York Daily News, February 25, 2002

The New York Times, March 15 and 17, 2002

Newsweek, November 12, 2001

People, March 25, 2002; June 2001

Planet Hollywood, June 2001

Popstar Magazine, February 2001

Premiere, February 2002

Teen, March 1998

TeenPeople, February 2002

The Hartford Courant, February 24, 2002

The New Yorker, March 11, 2002

Toronto Sun, August 31, 2001

Twist, March 2002

Star, September 18, 2001

Star Tribune, January 2002

Vanity Fair, June 2001

W, January 2002

World Entertainment News Network,
    May 16, 22, 29; June 1, 14, 18;
    August 29; December 29, 2001;
    February 29; March 1, 2002

YM Magazine, October 1997

WEBSITES YOU MIGHT WANT TO CHECK OUT

www.astrology-online.com

www.beautifulboy.com

www.dimensionfilms.com

www.eonline.com

www.habitat.org

www.hollywood.com

www.imdb.com

www.Josh-Hartnett.org

www.josh-hartnett.gq.nu

www.joshhartnett.net

www.m-w.com

www.movieline.com

www.moviething.com

www.nationalgeographic.com

www.starpulse.com

www.teenpeople.com

www.thespiannet.com

www.wenn.com

You can contact Josh at:

Josh Hartnett
Patricola/Lust
8271 Melrose Ave. #110
Los Angeles, CA 90046

"You aspire to be a good person first off, and a great actor second. There's no way to go about it. You just draw your own map."

PHOTO CREDITS